Grammar Success

Raising Writing Standards

Pie Corbett   Rachel Roberts

OXFORD

OXFORD
UNIVERSITY PRESS

Great Clarendon Street, Oxford OX2 6DP

Oxford University Press is a department of the University of Oxford.
It furthers the University's objective of excellence in research,
scholarship, and education by publishing worldwide in

Oxford New York

Athens Auckland Bangkok Bogotá Buenos Aires Calcutta
Cape Town Chennai Dar es Salaam Delhi Florence Hong Kong
Istanbul Karachi Kuala Lumpur Madrid Melbourne Mexico City
Mumbai Nairobi Paris São Paulo Singapore Taipei Tokyo
Toronto Warsaw

with associated companies in Berlin Ibadan

Oxford is a registered trade mark of Oxford University Press in the
UK and in certain other countries

© Oxford University Press 2000

ISBN 0 19 8342853

Typeset and designed by Oxford Designers & Illustrators, Oxford

Printed in Hong Kong

Preface

Grammar Success is about teaching children how to use grammar to improve their writing. It provides materials, not only to deepen children's grammatical understanding, but also to refine their grammatical skills and to enable them to apply these to their own writing.

The course is built around the National Literacy Framework sentence level objectives. However, where there are gaps in the framework (for instance, the omission of nouns from Year 3) these have been addressed. Each unit is each broken down into three sessions, based around the Pupils' Book, Teacher's Book and the Overhead Transparency Pack.

Session 1 uses an OHT to introduce the grammatical objective to the children. This part of the session should be lively, and interactive. Children then deepen their understanding of the particular grammatical feature through various independent activities. By the end of Session 1, pupils should be in a position to define their understanding of the objective.

Session 2 uses the Pupils' Book unit, plus photocopiable activities in the Teacher's Book. Pupils focus upon the grammatical feature in the context of wide-ranging stimulus texts. The children are asked comprehension questions on each text before moving into activities that focus upon the grammatical feature in use. By the end of this session, pupils have critically reflected upon the use of the objective through their reading.

Session 3 relates again to the text in the Pupils' Book, which now becomes a model for children's own writing. The teacher's notes describe in detail how to carry out shared writing, demonstrating how to use the grammatical feature in the process of writing a new text. A photocopiable Reminder Sheet in the Teacher's Book provides a summary, defining the grammatical feature and giving guidance on how to use it effectively in writing. It can be used for activities flagged by the symbol |R|. The session ends with pupils producing their own work, drawing on the shared writing experience.

While a full range of texts and outcomes are provided in the Pupils' Book, children will gain greater understanding of the grammar, if all three elements of the course are available to them.

Activities are differentiated in both Pupils' Book and Teacher's Book to allow for pupils who may struggle or who need an extra challenge. The photocopiable activities double as a valuable homework resource.

The course helps pupils to understand grammar but also to be come skilful in the key grammatical skills of:

- Sentence construction
- Punctuation
- Enhancing writing with different language effects
- Cohesion – links with and between sentences, paragraphs and texts.

The more adept children are at using these skills in their writing, the more freedom they will have to focus upon the act of creative composition.

Pie Corbett

Sources

The texts used in this book are extracted from the following full sources, and we are grateful for their permission to reproduce copyright material.

p 6   From BBC Factfinders: *Invaders* by Peter Chrisp, copyright © Peter Chrisp 1997, reproduced by permission of BBC Worldwide Limited.

p 8   From *The Whales' Song* by Dyan Sheldon, illustrated by Gary Blythe (Hutchinson 1990, Red Fox 1993), reproduced by permission of The Random House Group Ltd on behalf of Dyan Sheldon.

p 10   From *The Life of a Car* (New Horizons School Science Series, 1994), reprinted by permission of the publisher, Cambridge University Press.

p 12   'Greedy Dog' by James Hurley from *If you Should Meet a Crocodile* (Kaye & Ward 1974), copyright © James Hurley 1974.

p 14   From *A Gift from Winklesea* by Helen Cresswell (1969), reprinted by permission of the publisher, Hodder & Stoughton Ltd.

p 16   'Battle', first published here, copyright © Pie Corbett 2000.

p 18   'Going Bowling', first published here, copyright © Rachel Roberts 2000.

p 20   'Cat in the Window' by Brian Morse from *Picnic on the Moon* (Piper Books), reprinted by permission of the author.

p 22   'Jack and Wily Fox', first published here, copyright © Pie Corbett 2000.

p 24   From *Revolting Recipes* by Roald Dahl (Jonathan Cape, 1994), copyright © Felicity Dahl and Roald Dahl Nominee Ltd 1994, reprinted by permission of The Random House Group Ltd; illustration by Quentin Blake, copyright © Quentin Blake 1994, reprinted by permission of AP Watt Ltd on behalf of Roald Dahl Nominee Ltd.

p 26   'The Strange Room', first published here, copyright © Pie Corbett 2000.

p 28   From *Kensuke's Kingdom* by Michael Morpurgo (Egmont Children's Books, 1999), reprinted by permission of David Higham Associates; from 'Stone Soup' by Mike Dunstan in *Tales, Myths and Legends* edited by Pie Corbett (Scholastic); and from interview with Brian Moses in *Interviews with Writers* edited by James Carter (Routledge).

p 30   Extracted from 'Milk Notes from Story Street' by Tony Mitton, copyright © Tony Mitton 1994, first published in *Mrs Noah's Notebook and Other Kinds of Writing* compiled by Brian Moses (OUP, 1994), reprinted by permission of the author.

p 32   'My Dad, Your Dad' by Kit Wright from *Rabbiting On, and Other Poems* (Fontana Young Lions, 1978), reprinted by permission of the author; illustration by Posy Simmonds reprinted by permission of PFD.

p 34   From *The Vanishment of Thomas Tull* by Janet and Allan Ahlberg, (Puffin, 1985), copyright © Janet and Allan Ahlberg 1977, reprinted by permission of Penguin Books Ltd.

p 36   Adapted from *William and the Ghost* by Mike Poulton (Oxford Reading Tree, OUP, 1988), reprinted by permission of OUP, illustration by Alex Brychta, copyright © Alex Brychta 1988, reprinted by permission of the illustrator.

p 38   From *The Suitcase Kid* by Jacqueline Wilson (Doubleday, a division of Transworld Publishing, 1992), copyright © Jacqueline Wilson 1992, and from *Dinosaur's Packed Lunch* (Doubleday, a division of Transworld Publishing, 1995), copyright © Jacqueline Wilson 1995, both reprinted by permission of Transworld Publishers, a division of the Random House Group Ltd. All rights reserved.

p 40   'I'm The Youngest in Our House' by Michael Rosen, reprinted by permission of PFD on behalf of the author.

p 42   From Oxford Junior Dictionary (3rd edition, OUP 1995), reprinted by permission of Oxford University Press.

p 44   From *Dear Greenpeace* by Simon James (1991), copyright © Simon James 1991, reprinted by permission of the publisher, Walker Books Ltd, London.

We would also like to thank the following for permission to reproduce photographs:
Jorvik Viking Centre for Viking reconstruction and Viking jewellery.
Bob Battersby for Battle Abbey.
Bob Mazzer and the *Rye and Battle Observer* for Battle bonfire parade.

Although we have tried to trace and contact all copyright holders before publication this has not always been possible. If notified, we will be pleased to rectify any errors or omissions at the earliest opportunity.

Contents

TERM 1

UNIT

1	Reviewing the basics	Report	6
2	Speech punctuation	Story	8
3	Text presentation	Science textbook	10
4	Using verbs	Poem	12
5	Story verbs	Story	14
6	Verbs in reports	Report	16
7	Question & exclamation marks	Playscript	18

TERM 2

UNIT

8	Using nouns	Poem	20
9	Singular & plural nouns	Story	22
10	Capital letters	Recipe	24
11	Adjectives	Adventure story	26
12	1st, 2nd or 3rd person	Story	28
13	Key words for meaning	Instruction poem	30
14	Commas	Poem	32

TERM 3

UNIT

15	Grammatical agreement	Story	34
16	Joining sentences	Adventure story	36
17	Personal pronouns	Story	38
18	Using dialogue	Poem	40
19	Making longer sentences	Dictionary	42
20	Pronouns & possessive pronouns	Letters	44

Reviewing the basics

VIKING SETTLERS

The Vikings were not just fierce warriors. They were also farmers, traders and craftworkers, just like the Anglo-Saxons. The Vikings settled down to farm and to trade in the Danelaw in England, Scotland, Ireland and the Isle of Man.

Place names tell us where the Vikings settled in Britain. Viking ones often end in *by*, *thorpe*, *dale*, *waite* and *toft*. There are hundreds of these names in the north and east of Britain, but almost none in the south-west. Like Anglo-Saxon place names, Viking ones often include the name of the man who first settled there. For example Grimsby, Gaddesby and Kettleby were settled by Vikings called *Grim*, *Gad* and *Ketil*.

One of the most important Viking settlements was at York, which the Vikings called Jorvik. Merchants from Denmark and Norway sailed up the River Ouse to Jorvik bringing goods such as slaves, furs and amber. In Jorvik the craftworkers made beautiful jewellery such as amber necklaces and metal brooches.

(based on *Invaders*, BBC Factfinders)

Read through the text and discuss the following questions.

1 From which countries did the Vikings come to Britain?

2 List four things which the text tells you that the Vikings did.

3 Find 10 places in your area which may have been founded by Vikings.

4 How do you think the people in York felt about the Vikings who came to live there?

5 Lists involve two or more items. Complete the following chart.

Items in list	Commas	Example from text
two three four five		

6 What is the quickest way to find lists in the text?

7 Rewrite these sentences, adding lists to complete them.
Britain has been invaded by many groups of people such as…
My favourite sandwich fillings are…
Potatoes can be cooked in many ways, for example…

8 Find an example of a sentence divided into two parts by a comma. Rewrite it as two separate sentences.

9 List the different punctuation marks in this passage, and explain why they are used.

10 Write a brief report about the area in which you live for a website aimed at seven and eight year olds.

Remember to use commas correctly, if you include any lists in your report.

7

Speech punctuation

The Whales' Song

Lilly's grandmother has been telling her about the whales that used to swim in the ocean near her home…

*L*ILLY'S Grandmother smiled. 'Oh, you had to bring them something special. A perfect shell. Or a beautiful stone. And if they liked you the whales would take your gift and give you something in return.'

'What would they give you, Grandma?' asked Lilly. 'What did you get from the whales?'

Lilly's grandmother sighed. 'Once or twice,' she whispered, 'once or twice I heard them sing.'

Lilly's uncle Frederick stomped into the room. 'You're nothing but a daft old fool!' he snapped. 'Whales were important for their meat, and for their bones and for their blubber. If you have to tell Lilly something, then tell her something useful. Don't fill her head with nonsense. Singing whales indeed!'

'There were whales here millions of years before there were ships, or cities, or even cavemen,' continued Lilly's grandmother. 'People used to say they were magical.'

'People used to eat them and boil them down for oil!' grumbled Lilly's uncle Frederick. And he turned his back and stomped out into the garden.

Dyan Sheldon and Gary Blythe

Read through the extract and discuss the following questions.

1 How does Lilly's grandmother feel about whales?

2 What does she believe she heard from the whales?

3 What kind of mood is she in?

4 What does Lilly's uncle Frederick think that whales should be used for?

5 Is Lilly's uncle Frederick in a good mood or not? How do you know?

6 Look at the three characters in the extract. Find the speech verbs used for each character and make a list of them like this.

Lilly:	Grandmother:	Uncle Frederick:
	sighed	

7 Lilly's friend, Simon comes for tea.

Lilly and Simon are talking about whales when her uncle and grandmother come in.

Continue the conversation between the four characters. You might start like this.

> *'Have you ever seen a whale, Lilly?' asked Simon.*
> *'No,' said Lilly, 'but I wish I had. My Grandma has, though. She's even heard them sing!'*
> *'Wow! That must have been really great. Do you think we could hear them too, Lilly?'*
> *Lilly's Grandmother and uncle Frederick walked in.*

Staying on the Road

Have you noticed how a car glides smoothly along a road? It does not bump or jolt. This is partly due to the tyres. It is also due to the springs and dampers which make up the car's **suspension system**.

The suspension system

It would be very uncomfortable to drive in a car with no springs. It would also be dangerous. The car would jump about every time it hit a bump or rut. The tyres would lose contact with the road and make steering and stopping difficult.

Springs absorb the shock by making the wheels bounce with the bumps.

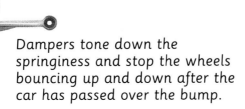

Dampers tone down the springiness and stop the wheels bouncing up and down after the car has passed over the bump.

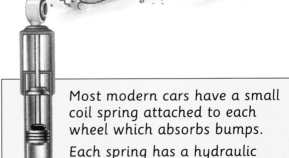

Most modern cars have a small coil spring attached to each wheel which absorbs bumps.

Each spring has a hydraulic damper. A piston forces fluid through tiny holes to control the bouncing movement of the spring.

Did you know...?

Before suspension systems had dampers, a car once jumped over a hedge when it hit a bump in the road.

Read this page from a Science textbook.

1 Which three parts of the car are the most important in keeping the car on the road?

2 Copy this table and complete it, using the information in the text.

Car part	What it does	What would happen if it wasn't there

3 Find two information texts. Look at the different ways in which each writer presents the text. Work out the reasons why they have done this, and put them in a table like the one below.

Type	Text 1	Reason why	Text 2	Reason why
Underlined				
Bold				
Italic				
Heading				
Sub-heading				
Caption				
Other				
Comment				

4 Write a caption about the materials used in building cars to include on a textbook page. You may need a copy of the page layout that the class has been working on. You will need to decide where on the page to place your caption.

If you have time, try writing a second caption.

Using verbs

Greedy Dog

This dog will eat anything.

Apple cores and bacon fat,
Milk you poured out for the cat.
He likes the string that ties the roast
And relishes hot buttered toast.
Hide your chocolates! He's a thief,
He'll even eat your handkerchief.
And if you don't like sudden shocks,
Carefully conceal your socks.
Leave some soup without a lid,
And you'll wish you never did.
When you think he must be full,
You find him gobbling bits of wool,
Orange peel or paper bags,
Dusters and old cleaning rags.

This dog will eat anything,
Except for mushrooms and cucumber.

Now what is wrong with those, I wonder?

James Hurley

Read through the poem and discuss the following questions.

1 Which word best describes this dog?
   hungry   thoughtless   stupid   greedy

2 Find one example that explains why the dog is called a thief.

3 How might he give you sudden shocks?

4 Why do you think that he does not eat mushrooms and cucumber?

5 How do you think the poet feels about the dog?

6 Read through the poem and list the three most powerful verbs that
   you can find. For example, to make the dog sound greedy, James
   Hurley has used the verb *gobbling*. Make a list of all the verbs that
   could be used instead of *eat*.

7 Rewrite the following lines from the poem by using a more powerful
   verb than *eat*.
   This dog will eat anything.
   He'll even eat your handkerchief!

8 Write a poem called *Lively Cat*, listing all the different things that
   your cat might do.

   Take care to choose powerful verbs. For example, you could begin
   your poem like this:

   This cat will do *anything.*

   She dozes *at the foot of my bed.*
   She purrs *when I stroke her.*
   She prowls *in the night.*
   She creeps *along wall tops.*

Story verbs

A GIFT FROM WINKLESEA

At that moment the egg, with a final acrobatic leap, jumped right clear of the pedestal and landed smack at the feet of the glass cat. Mary and Mrs Kane screamed together. Then, knives and forks poised in mid air, they saw that the egg was split right across. Slowly the gap between the two halves widened. They stared.

'Do something,' moaned Mrs Kane again. 'Quick, Alfred, do something.'

'Shush!' said Mr Kane. 'Watch!'

And as they watched, a most perfectly beautiful, neat grey little creature parted the stone shell and stepped out on to the polished tiles of the mantelpiece.

'It's a – it's a – what is it?' whispered Mrs Kane.

'It's a baby kangaroo!' said Mary.

It quite obviously was not, but as nobody else had the least idea what it was, nobody bothered to contradict her. Outside a factory siren began to hoot and they all jumped. Dan got up and went over to the mantelpiece.

'Dan!' cried Mrs Kane. 'Come away this minute!'

'It's all right, Mum,' he said, 'it won't bite. Look you've frightened it now.'

The Gift from Winklesea had gone behind the clock. It moved so swiftly that they hardly saw it go. 'Look at that!' exclaimed Mr Kane admiringly. 'Proper little greyhound!'

He too got up and went over. A small grey head and beady eye peered from behind the clock face.

'It's looking at us!' cried Mary. 'Isn't it sweet!'

'I don't know about sweet,' said Mrs Kane. But she, too, came over and joined them.

Helen Cresswell

Read through the extract and discuss the following questions.

1   How does Mrs Kane feel about what is happening?

2   How do you know?

3   What does Mr Kane think?

4   Which word tells you?

5   List three well-chosen speech verbs that have been used instead of *said*.

6   List three verbs that show that the story is written in the past – it has already happened.

7   Change these sentences to strengthen the verbs.
    Dan got up and went over to the mantelpiece.
    The Gift from Winklesea had gone behind the clock.
    It moved so swiftly that they hardly saw it go.
    'It's looking at us!'
    But she, too, came over and joined them.

8   Scan through any storybook and collect speech verbs to use in your writing.

9   Brainstorm a list of powerful verbs to use instead of:
    went   (She *went* across the road.)
    looked (She *looked* at it.)

10 What will happen next in the story, now that the small grey creature is out of its shell? Continue the conversation between Mr and Mrs Kane, Mary and Daniel.

    Remember to choose speech verbs that bring out the characters' feelings. Try to use the past tense for verbs and stick to it.

Verbs in reports

Battle

Battle is a small town.

It is situated in the south of England. It is six miles from the seaside town of Hastings.

The town has several thousand people living there. There are four pubs where you can eat. There are two churches as well as a primary and a secondary school. In the town there are all the shops that you need. There is a big supermarket but also lots of smaller shops. There is a bookshop and a small museum. The most interesting building is called Battle Abbey. This is built on the place where the famous Battle of Hastings was fought in 1066, against William the Conqueror.

There are lots of things that you can do in Battle. Each year on November the 5th there is a large bonfire in the middle of the town. Everyone dresses up and there is a large parade. The firework display is tremendous.

People who live in Battle like it. It is large enough to have lots of shops, and the abbey is interesting. But it is also small enough to know most people of your own age.

Read the report through carefully and discuss the following questions.

1 How far from the sea is Battle?

2 What is the most interesting building in the town?

3 Why is the town called Battle?

4 What is the most exciting event that happens each year?

5 Look at how the report is written. What does paragraph four tell the reader about?

6 List three verbs in the present tense. Change them to the past tense in a chart like this.

Verb used in present tense	Changed to past tense
is	was

7 Rewrite these sentences turning them into the present tense.
   The town was very small.
   There was a hospital on the edge of the town.
   The school had over 100 children.

8 Read through the report about Battle. Use the same structure to write five paragraphs about a place that you know really well. Plan what you will say first. Remember to use the present tense.

Question & exclamation marks

Going Bowling

Setting: at the bowling alley

James: Yes! Go on then – beat that!

Charlotte: OK, then. So you think you're the only one who can bowl?

Mel: Boys!

Charlotte: Everyone out of the way, here we go… …oh, there must've been something wrong with the ball. Did you see that, Mel? It was wonky. It definitely went wonky. That's not fair! I should have another go.

James: Can't take it, eh? Girls!

Mel: Let's just have one more go each, and then go and get a drink or something. You two have been arguing ever since we got here. This is supposed to be my birthday treat, you know.

Charlotte: Sorry, Mel. I just know I'm better than him. I always win. I'm going to have another go.

James: That's not fair, it's my turn now. You just can't take it, can you? You'll sulk now, I bet.

Charlotte: That ball was wonky – you saw it wobble didn't you, Mel? Mel? James – where's Mel?

Read the playscript extract and discuss the following questions.

1 Why are the children at the bowling alley?

2 Why is Charlotte upset?

3 How does James feel about this?

4 Where do you think Mel goes at the end?

5 Explain why you think Mel has left.

6 Write out at least four examples of sentences with exclamation marks from the extract. Next to them, write how each character feels as they say each sentence. For example:

1 *Yes*! (James – proud)

7 Look at the questions in the playscript. There is really only one question here where the speaker does not know the answer. Which is it? Copy it out. Then write down some reasons why the characters ask the other questions.

IR

8 What will happen next in the play? Will Charlotte and James find Mel? Will James' and Charlotte's moods change? Continue the playscript.

Remember to include stage directions and punctuation that will help show the characters' feelings. As you write, think carefully about how you set out the script.

UNIT 8 *Using nouns*

CAT IN THE WINDOW

Cat in the window,
  what do you see?

Cloud, wind, leaves,
  a bird in a tree.

The daffodils shivering
  in the February breeze,

A puddle in the road
  beginning to freeze.

Snow on the wind,
  dusk in a cloud,

Leaves in a frenzy,
  the bird's head cowed.

Winter – though the sun shines.
  Blizzard, and the north wind's whine.

Brian Morse

Read through the text and discuss the following questions.

1 Which word suggests that the daffodils are cold?

2 What time of day is it in verse 5?

3 Which three clues tell you that the weather is bad?

4 How do you think the cat feels? Give your reasons.

5 List 15 nouns from the poem.

6 Make the picture of the poem stronger for the reader by naming the particular type of:

Cat:

Bird:

Tree:

7 List five other nouns that the cat would see from your classroom window.

8 You are going to write a poem based on *Cat in the Window*. Look back over the poem and decide which animal you will be. What will you notice from the window? For example, the cat is interested in the bird in the tree.

Remember to choose the nouns precisely to create a strong picture of what your animal sees.

Singular & plural nouns

Jack and the Wily Fox

It was not long after the giant crashed down the beanstalk into the garden, just missing the cottage roof, that Jack's mother told Jack to go to the market to spend some money.

'The farmyard is almost empty. Go to the market and buy some more animals. And this time do not swap them for a handful of beans!'

So off goes Jack down the lane towards the market. On the way he stopped for his lunch. He was sitting on a bank of moss and leaves when along came a little old man.

'I'm so hungry,' said the old man, 'that I'll swap your lunch for these cows, my pigs and sheep.'

But Jack he knows what his mother told him, so he shakes his head and hurries on his way to the city, and down to the market.

Well, sooner rather than later back comes Jack. He has a grin as wide as the sky. On the end of a rope he has plenty of animals for the farmyard. Jack's mother can hear them coming up the lane. Such a hooting, a roaring, a bellowing you never would believe it was true.

'Here you are mother, I've brought two of each animal I saw at the market, as well as some I collected on the way. I've got dogs, cats, horses, foxes, fishes, flies, ducks, geese, chickens, bunnies, wolves, sheep, a swarm of bees, a pride of lions and a herd of cattle.'

All went well for a while. That was until one of the chickens got too close to one of the foxes. The temptation was too much. The fox leaped after the chicken, the dogs chased the fox, the lions chased the foxes and then one of the cows trod on the bees. You should have heard the racket. Those bees, they stung everything in sight!

Read the story through and discuss the following questions.

1 Suggest a reason why Jack should have swapped his lunch for the cows, pigs and sheep.

2 Give two reasons why he has a *grin as wide as the sky*.

3 Why does the fox chase the chicken?

4 What do you think Jack's mother is going to say to him?

5 What advice would you give Jack for the next time he goes to market?

6 Complete a chart like the one below, by finding three words in the story that fit into each column. Write in both the singular and the plural for each word.

Singular	Plural ends in 's'	Singular	Plural end in 'ies'	Singular	Plural ends in 'ves'
		ends in 'y'		ends in 'f'	

Singular	Plural ends in 'es'	Singular	Odd plurals
ends in 'ch', 'ss', 'sh', 'x'			

7 Copy out what Jack says to his mother when he gets back from the market. Change all the plurals into singular nouns. Try to get the spelling right, using the chart.

8 There are many stories about Jack. Sometimes they feature Mary. Mary is usually cleverer than Jack. Write another sequel to *Jack and the Beanstalk* in which Jack gets sent to buy something. What does he buy this time and what happens to him? Will your story include Mary or Jack's mother?

Remember to check the spelling of plural words, using what you have discovered about different plurals.

Capital letters

WONKA'S NUTTY CRUNCH SURPRISE

From Charlie and the Chocolate Factory

YOU WILL NEED:

pyrex bowl
saucepan
8 x 10 inch (20 x 25 cm)
shallow tin, greased and lined
with greaseproof paper
greaseproof paper

7oz (200g) plain chocolate,
broken into small pieces
2oz (50g) butter
5 tbsp (75ml) golden syrup
6oz (175g) Rich Tea biscuits,
finely crushed
3oz (75g) flaked almonds
1oz (25g) Rice Crispies
a few drops of vanilla essence

FOR THE NUTTY
CRUNCH:

2oz (50g) flaked almonds, finely
chopped
4oz (100g) granulated sugar
(cane)
2tbsp (30ml) water

FOR THE CHOCOLATE
COATING:

7oz (200g) milk chocolate,
broken into small pieces

1 Put the chocolate, butter and golden syrup in a pyrex bowl and place over a saucepan of simmering water. Stir occasionally until melted. Alternatively place in microwave oven and cook on high for $1^1/_2$ minutes.

2 Add the almonds, crushed biscuits, Rice Crispies and vanilla essence and mix well.

3 Spoon the mixture into the lined tin and press down firmly with the back of a fork, creating a level surface.

4 Allow to cool in the fridge, then cut into bars.

5 Then make the nutty crunch; begin by placing the water and sugar into a small saucepan. Leave on a low heat until the sugar has dissolved. Do not stir, but occasionally swirl the pan around gently. Increase the heat and continue stirring until the sugar caramelizes and turns golden brown, approx 2-3 minutes.

6 Remove from the heat, add the chopped almonds, and working quickly, stir thoroughly and dip one end of the bars in the mixture. Place the bars on a sheet of buttered greaseproof paper to set.

7 Melt the chocolate in the pyrex bowl, over a saucepan of simmering water, or microwave. Once it has melted, remove from the heat and dip the opposite end of each bar in the chocolate.

8 Leave to cool on a sheet of greaseproof paper or non-stick silicon paper.

From *Revolting Recipes,* by Roald Dahl (Jonathan Cape, 1994).

Read through the recipe and discuss the following questions.

1 This recipe was mentioned in a story book. What is its title?

2 What time of day might you eat Nutty Crunch Surprise?

3 Why has the writer used sub-headings?

4 Suggest one way in which this recipe might be improved.

5 Read the recipe and other pieces of information that go with it. Then make a list of all the words with a capital letter. Decide why they have been used and write a reason beside each example. Two examples have been done for you.

Word with a capital	Reason for capital letter
NUTTY	It's part of the title
Charlie	It's someone's name

See how many different reasons you can find in this text.

6 Skim through other extracts in this book and find any different reasons for using a capital letter. Add the word with its page number to your list and a reason why a capital has been used.

7 You are going to write a set of instructions for a playground game. Choose a game that you know well. The instructions are for someone who has never played the game before, so make sure that they are simple and clear. You may need diagrams to help the reader.

Adjectives

THE STRANGE ROOM

The Prince strode into the room. He marched across the carpet and grabbed hold of Tamara's arm.

'You must do as I say,' he snapped at her.

'Ouch!' yelled Tamara. 'You are hurting me.'

'I don't care,' growled the Prince angrily. 'I cannot be kept waiting. We have to escape immediately.'

There was a sudden click in the lock. The Prince stared in fury. How dare they be locked in! It was then that for the first time he looked around the room they were in. On the large, broken table laid a disgusting meal. There were cracked plates piled high with rotting grapes, mouldy puddings and stale grey bread. There was a jug of cold, yellow tea.

The damp walls of the room were made of jagged, purple stone. A small, worn carpet covered the cold, dark floorboards. On the walls there were dusty paintings of kings and queens long since dead. In one painting there was a thin, pale dragon sleeping. Bending over the dragon was a man very much like himself. Is this my father, wondered the Prince?

The Prince then noticed a plate piled high with green emeralds and glittering diamonds. Perhaps it was here that he would find the crystal that he had been seeking. However, at that very moment, there was a tap on the window.

Read through the passage and discuss the following questions.

1 Find two clues that tell us that the Prince is a bully.

2 Which words suggest that the Prince might be a soldier?

3 What does the Prince think when the door is locked?

4 Find two things that the Prince is searching for.

5 Is the Prince right to be angry?

6 Make a list of the nouns and their adjectives in paragraphs two and three. The adjectives make the meal sound disgusting and the room rather uninviting.

List different adjectives that would make the meal sound worth eating and the room sound bright and cheerful.

7 List your adjectives under three different headings. Add other possible adjectives to the list.

Colour	Size	Look
red	large	dull
blue	small	dirty

IR

8 Decide what might happen next in the story. Note down two or three possible incidents. Each incident can be turned into a paragraph.

Continue with the story, selecting adjectives with care. Remember that only some nouns will need an adjective. Keep the character of the Prince the same unless something happens to change him. What else might you include about Tamara's character?

1st, 2nd or 3rd person

Three Descriptions

A

He had holes in the knees of his trousers, his boots were coming apart, the tops from the bottoms (he'd tried to mend them by wrapping Sellotape around to hold them together), his overcoat was tied around the middle by a piece of old rope and perched on his head was a battered old felt hat.

Mike Dunstan

B

This girl had a budgie that her dad accidentally sucked up into the vacuum cleaner when he was cleaning out the cage. So they got the budgie out of the dust bag, and the budgie was a bit dusty and he was coughing a lot. So they washed him and put him back on his perch, and the next day he was fine.

Brian Moses

C

I sat up. I was on a beach, a broad white sweep of sand, with trees growing thick and lush behind me right down to the beach. Then I saw Stella prancing about in the shallows. I called her and she came bounding up out of the sea to greet me, her tail circling wildly. When all the leaping and licking and hugging were done, I struggled to my feet.

I was weak all over. I looked about me. The wide blue sea was as empty as the cloudless sky above. No *Peggy Sue*. No boat. Nothing. No one. I called again and again for my mother and my father. I called until the tears came and I could call no more, until I knew there was no point.

(From *Kensuke's Kingdom* by Michael Morpurgo)

Read through extracts A, B and C and discuss the following questions.

1 What type of writing does each extract come from?

2 What clues can you find to support your ideas?

3 What sort of person is described in extract A?

4 Do you believe extract B – what is the strangest tale you have heard?

5 In extract C, who or what is *Stella*?

6 Who or what is *Peggy Sue*?

7 What has happened to the character in extract C?

8 Rewrite extract A, changing it from 3rd to 1st person, as if you were writing your diary or a letter to a friend about how ragged you looked. *I had holes in the knees of my trousers…*

9 Keep the writing in the 1st person and add some extra description to your writing. You could include a pair of torn trousers, broken glasses, a ripped shirt, a threadbare jumper, and in your hand a battered suitcase.

10 Read extract C again and rewrite it in the 3rd person, as if it were a story. Continue with the next few paragraphs in the 3rd person. What might the storyteller do next? What else might Stella do?

Key words for meaning

(From *Notes for the Milkman* by Tony Mitton)

1 Match each note (A–H) to the correct address from the list below (1–8).

> ### The milkman's delivery list
>
> 1 The Owl and the Pussycat, Honeysuckle House
> 2 Snow White and the Seven Dwarfs, Wood Cottage
> 3 The Grand Old Duke of York, Military Mansions
> 4 The Cat with the Fiddle, The Dish and Spoon Public House
> 5 Jack Sprat and Spouse, The Wide Cottage with the Narrow Windows
> 6 Tom Thumb, Shoebox Dwelling (tread carefully)
> 7 Jack and Jill, The House under the Hill
> 8 The Old Woman who lived in a Shoe, no number, but you can't mistake it

2 Some of these notes could be shorter. The milkman has no time to waste in reading long notes. See how many words you can cut from notes C, E, G and H, without losing any information that the milkman needs to know.

3 Write a telegram from a well-known fairy tale character, asking for help. Each word costs £1 to send so you can only have up to 30 words. See whose telegram can be the briefest.
- Goldilocks to a friend when she is stuck in the three bears' cottage
- Red Riding Hood to her mother when she is at grandma's house
- The first Billy Goat Gruff to his brothers once he is across the bridge
- Jack to his mother when the giant is chasing him
- Cinderella to a friend when the others have gone to the ball

My Dad, Your Dad

My dad's fatter than your dad,
Yes, my dad's fatter than yours:
If he eats any more he won't fit in the house,
He'll have to live out of doors.

Yes, but my dad's balder than your dad,
My dad's balder, OK,
He's only got two hairs left on his head
And both are turning grey.

Ah, but my dad's thicker than your dad,
My dad's thicker, all right.
He has to look at his watch to see
If it's noon or the middle of the night.

Yes, but my dad's more boring than your dad.
If he ever starts counting sheep
When he can't get to sleep at night, he finds
It's the sheep that go to sleep.

But my dad doesn't mind your dad.
Mine quite likes yours too.
I suppose they don't always think much of US!
That's true, I suppose, that's true.

Kit Wright

Read through the poem and discuss the following questions.

1 Why do you think the two speakers are boasting about their dads?

2 How big is the fat dad?

3 How thick is the thick dad?

4 How many hairs has the bald dad got left?

5 What do the two dads think of each other?

6 In each verse of the poem which two lines rhyme?

7 What sorts of things might the dads say about the children?

8 Work in pairs to prepare a reading for the class. As you practise reading, be careful to pause at the commas and stop at full stops. Try reading the poem with and without the pauses. Be ready to read the poem in class.

9 Use Kit Wright's poem as a model to write some more funny boasts that the two dads might make about the children. Decide if they are talking about their daughters or sons. Are they thinner, smaller, taller, shorter, quieter, louder, quicker, slower or funnier than the other dad's child?

Copy this pattern, including the commas, to help you write your poem.

My son's............than your son,
Yes, my son's............than yours:
If he gets any............ ,
He'll............ .

UNIT 15

Grammatical agreement

The Vanishment of Thomas Tull

When Thomas Tull was seven years old he stopped growing, which was bad, and began shrinking, which was worse. By the time he was seven and a half none of his clothes fitted him at all; and when his eighth birthday arrived he had to stand on a box to blow his candles out.

Mr and Mrs Tull were much upset by the slow disappearance of their son. In the beginning Mrs Tull said, 'That boy just needs to eat more. Eating makes you grow, it is a proven fact!'

'Yes dear,' said Mr Tull, and went out to hire a chef.

Allan Ahlberg

Read the extract and discuss the following questions.

1 What sort of text is this?

2 Could the things that happen to Thomas Tull really happen?

3 List the things that could happen and the things that could not.

4 How do you think Thomas feels about shrinking?

5 Here are some sentences about Thomas Tull. The verbs have been left out. Write them down, making the verbs agree grammatically. Complete the third sentence in your own words.
   Thomas Tull… seven when he… growing.
   Thomas Tull's parents… very worried about him.
   If I… Thomas Tull's parent, I would… .

6 Look at the opening page of your reading book. In each paragraph, list how many times the writer uses names for characters and how many times they use pronouns. Fill in the following table. An example from *The Vanishment of Thomas Tull* has been done for you.

Paragraph	Name	Pronouns
1 Thomas Tull		he (3); his (2)
2 Mr and Mrs Tull	Mrs Tull	

7 Make sure you can see the story-board that the class has been working on.
   • Carry on writing the story, using the four frames to help you.
   • Read through your writing to make sure the verbs agree grammatically.

8 When you have finished the opening, swap your work with a partner.
   • Ask them what they think about it.
   • What do they like?
   • What would they do to make it better?

Joining sentences

William and the Ghost

Suddenly William shivered. 'It's gone cold in this room,' he thought.
He looked at his drawing. Then he looked at the armour. He began
to feel rather strange. The arm of the suit of armour had moved. As
William watched, a small door began to open at the back of the fire-
place. Out of the door came a little white dog.

The dog barked, looked at William and walked to the door in the
fire-place.

'Do you want to show me something?' asked William. The dog
wagged its tail. William followed it through the door and found
himself in a dark passage. In the passage were some stone steps.
William went down the steps and into a dark damp tunnel. He could
see light behind a door at the end of it. The little dog looked back to
make sure that William was following, and went through the door.

(adapted from the *Oxford Reading Tree* story by Mike Poulton)

Read the story extract and discuss the following questions.

1 What do you think William is drawing?

2 Why is he drawing it?

3 Where do you think the dog might have come from?

4 If you were William, what would you have done? Explain why.

5 The writer has used some short sentences and some long sentences in this extract. Read the following pairs of sentences and see if you can make each pair into one sentence. Use connecting words like *and*, *but*, *because* or *when* to do this.

He looked at his drawing. Then he looked at the armour.

He began to feel rather strange. The arm of the suit of armour had moved.

The dog wagged its tail. William followed it through the door.

6 Continue writing the story of *William and the Ghost*. What happens to him on the other side of the door? Plan out the events and write an ending for the story.

Remember to use connecting words to vary the length of sentences. Different sentence lengths help to keep the reader's interest going.

Personal pronouns

The Suitcase Kid

Graham and Katie and I go to the sweet shop.

'Hello, my darlings,' Mr Roberts says as soon as he sees us. He's always twinkling and stroking his beard. You expect him to go Ho-ho-ho like Father Christmas.

Graham is very shy with most people, but he gets quite chatty with Mr Roberts. But it's Katie who's the favourite. Naturally. She twirls about the shop like a sugar-plum fairy and Mr Roberts chuckles and claps and calls her his Little Precious and his Cute Little Sweetheart. He always lets her have a free go in his Lucky Bag, five pence a dip.

He offers me a free go but I just stick my nose in the air and say no thanks. I have to buy my sweets and chocolate from him because there's nowhere else to get it, but I'm not going to make friends.

Mr Roberts and I are deadly enemies.

Jacqueline Wilson

Read the extract and discuss the following questions.

1 How many children are there altogether?

2 What do you think Graham is like? Explain how you know.

3 What do you think Katie is like? Explain how you know.

4 What do you think Mr Roberts is like?

5 How does the narrator feel about Mr Roberts? Why might this be?

6 This extract is written in the 1st person. We can tell this because the writer has used the words *I* and *we*.

Here are some sentences from *The Dinosaur's Packed Lunch* by Jacqueline Wilson. They are written in the 3rd person. Rewrite them in the 1st person.
Dinah did not feel like breakfast.
Not cornflakes and milk.
'Boring,' said Dinah.
She made herself a jam sandwich.
'Yummy,' said Dinah, rubbing her tummy.
Dinah fed the teddy on her nightie, too.

7 Rewrite this extract as if you were Graham or Katie. What will you say about Mr Roberts? What will you reveal about the original narrator?

Remember to write in the 1st person and to use pronouns in place of nouns and proper nouns to make your story clear and readable.

Using dialogue

I'm the Youngest in our House

I'm the youngest in our house
so it goes like this:

My brother comes in and says:
'Tell him to clear the fluff
out from under his bed.'
Mum says,
'Clear the fluff
out from under your bed.'
Father says,
'You heard what your mother said.'
'What?' I say.
'The fluff,' he says.
'Clear the fluff
out from under your bed.'
So I say,
'There's fluff under his bed, too,
you know.'
So father says,
'But we're talking about the fluff
under your bed.'
'You will clear it up
won't you?' mum says.
So now my brother — all puffed up —
Says,
'Clear the fluff
out from under your bed.'
Now I'm angry. I am angry.
So I say — what shall I say?
I say,
'Shuttup Stinks
YOU CAN'T RULE MY LIFE.'

Michael Rosen

Read the poem and discuss the following questions.

1 How many children do you think there are in this family? Explain your answer.

2 Why does the brother become *all puffed up*? What does this mean?

3 In the last line, the writer says, *YOU CAN'T RULE MY LIFE.* Who is he talking to? How do you think he is feeling.

4 Write five words the writer might use to tell people what his older brother is like.

5 Here are some sentences which are not in standard English. Write them out correctly. The first four come from the poem, so you can use the text to check your answers.
My brother come in and say:
So fathers says,
Now I's angry.
YOUS CAN'T RULE MY LIFE.

He like apple pie.
They is no happy
We is going home.

6 Write about this argument as if you were the writer's brother. You do not need to write a poem.

Remember you will need to use the pronouns *I* and *me* and to use correct punctuation for the characters' speeches.

Making longer sentences

a b c d e f g h i j k l m n o **p q** r s t u v w x y z

pupil *noun* **pupils**
1 someone who has a teacher.
2 the black spot at the centre of the eye.

puppet *noun* **puppets**
a kind of doll, with a head and limbs that you can move by pulling strings or wires, or by fitting it over your hand like a glove.

puppy *noun* **puppies**
a very young dog.

pure *adjective* **purer, purest**
with nothing else mixed with it. *pure water.*

purple *noun, adjective*
a colour, between red and blue.

purpose *noun* **purposes**
what someone means to do.
on purpose deliberately, not by accident. *I didn't push you on purpose.*

purposely *adverb*
on purpose.

purr *verb* **purrs, purring, purred**
to make the sound a cat makes when it is very pleased.

purse *noun* **purses**
a small bag for holding money.

pursue *verb* **pursues, pursuing, pursued**
to go after someone and try to catch them.

push *verb* **pushes, pushing, pushed**
to use your hands to move something away from you.

pussy *noun* **pussies**
(*informal*) a cat or kitten.

put *verb* **puts, putting, put**
to move something to a place, to leave something in a place. *Please put the book back on the shelf.*
to put something off to decide to do it later instead of now.

to put up with something to let it happen without complaining even if you don't like it.

puzzle *noun* **puzzles**
a problem or question that is hard to solve. *a jigsaw puzzle.*

puzzle *verb* **puzzles, puzzling, puzzled**
to make you think hard to find the answer. *The riddle puzzled me.*

pyjamas *noun*
trousers and a jacket worn in bed.

pylon *noun* **pylons**
a metal tower that holds up high electric cables.

pyramid *noun* **pyramids**
1 a large, stone building made by the ancient Egyptians to hold the body of a dead king or queen.
2 the shape of a pyramid.

Qq

quack *verb* **quacks, quacking, quacked**
to make the sound a duck makes.

quaint *adjective* **quainter, quaintest**
unusual but pleasant. *a quaint cottage.*

quake *verb* **quakes, quaking, quaked**
to shake because you are very frightened. *She was quaking with fear.*

qualify *verb* **qualifies, qualifying, qualified**
1 to pass a test or exam so that you are allowed to do something.

Oxford Junior Dictionary

Read the dictionary page and answer the following questions.

1 Rewrite the definition of *purse* in your own words.

2 Which word would you use if you were writing about electricity?

3 Write a definition of the word *pushchair*.

4 Where would the word *pushchair* slot in on the page? Write down the word before it and the word which would go after it.

5 Look at the definitions of *purple* and *purr* on the dictionary page. In a chart like this one, write down which part of the definition is which. A different example has been done for you.

Word	Description	Detail
purse	a small bag	for holding money

On your chart underline the verbs in each sentence in red.

6 Now choose two of these definitions from the extract to add to the chart.

puppet   *push*   *quake*   *qualify*

7 Work in pairs to write a glossary for your current science topic.
   • First, draw up a list of key words.
   • Write each word onto a slip of paper. Then write a definition for that word.
   • Remember the structure of the definition: it should begin with a simple description, and then add some detail.
   • Finally, put the slips of paper into alphabetical order and stick the definitions down onto a page.
   If you wish, you could use a computer to write the definitions, and then organize them into alphabetical order using the 'cut' and 'paste' commands.

Pronouns & possessive pronouns

Dear Greenpeace

Dear Greenpeace,

Last night I read your letter to my whale. Afterwards he let me stroke his head. It was very exciting.

I secretly took him some crunched-up cornflakes and bread-crumbs. This morning I looked in the pond and they were all gone!

I think I shall call him Arthur what do you think?

Love
Emily

Dear Emily,

I must point out to you quite forcibly now that in no way could a whale live in your pond. You may not know that whales are migratory, which means they travel great distances each day.

I am sorry to disappoint you.

Yours sincerely,

Greenpeace

Read both letters and discuss the following questions.

1 How old do you think Emily is? Give a reason for your answer.

2 Why do you think Emily is writing to Greenpeace?

3 If you were Emily, what would you do about the reply?

4 What do Greenpeace think of Emily? Explain your answer.

5 Rewrite the first three sentences of Emily's letter without using pronouns. What effect does this have on the meaning?

6 Both letters contain possessive pronouns. Copy the chart below. Then complete it.

Line from letter	Possessive pronoun	Word(s) pronoun replaces

IR

7 Write a letter to a friend that tells them about something funny that has happened to you at school. Remember to start off with your address and the date you are writing on.

You could follow this plan, if you wish.

Paragraph 1: greeting – say hello and tell them what you have been doing since you last wrote
Paragraph 2: explain that something funny has happened at school
Paragraph 3: describe what happened
Paragraph 4: explain why it is so funny
Paragraph 5: ask your friend to write back
Paragraph 6: say goodbye and sign off with your name

When you finish the letter, check that you have used pronouns correctly.

Glossary

adjective   An adjective is a word that describes somebody or something. They usually come in front of a noun. For example:
green emeralds and *glittering* diamonds
a *thin, pale* dragon

agreement   Agreement is the link between the subject of a sentence and the verb. For example:
I am/I was
You are/you were
The boy was shrinking.
The boys were growing.

bold   Letters or words can be written in bold print, which is darker than normal. It can help to highlight words for the reader. For example:
… the car's **suspension system**.

capital letter   A capital letter starts the first word of a new sentence. It can be used to highlight words for the reader. For example:
YOU CAN'T RULE MY LIFE.

caption   A caption is a short sentence or phrases used with a picture. For example:
Springs absorb the shock by making the wheels bounce with the bumps.

comma   A comma (,) is a punctuation mark used to help the reader. It separates parts of sentences. It helps the reader take a pause when reading. For example:
That's true, I suppose, that's true.
One of the most important Viking settlements was at York, which the Vikings called Jorvik.

Commas are used when writing items in a list. For example:
Merchants sailed up the River Ouse to Jorvik bringing goods such as slaves, furs and amber.

connective   A connective is a word or phrase that provides a link within a sentence or between sentences. For example:
and, so, but, when, because, at first, next, finally

definition   A definition is an explanation of the meaning of a word. For example:
purse a small bag for holding money.

dialogue   Dialogue is the term used to describe a written conversation between two or more people. (See pages 8 and 14.)

exclamation mark   An exclamation mark (!) is a punctuation mark used to end an exclamation of joy, wonder, anger, surprise. For example:
That's not fair!

full stop	A full stop (.) is a punctuation mark most commonly used at the end of a sentence. For example: *Battle is a small town.*
heading	A heading is a title that is used to show the reader what a paragraph or section of text is about. For example: **The suspension system**
instruction	An instruction is a text written to help readers be able to accomplish a certain goal. For example: *Please start delivering as from today.*
italic	Italic writing is a handwriting style that slopes. It can be used to help highlight words for the reader. For example: Viking names often end in *by, thorpe.*
noun	A noun is a word that names something or somebody. For example: *fox, chicken, brother, rock, sea, cloud, picture, etc.*
performance poetry	This is a form of poetry that can be performed aloud, often with music or a number of readers. (See pages 32 and 40.)
person (1st, 2nd, or 3rd person)	1st person is used to talk about oneself – *I/we.* 2nd person is used to talk about whoever is listening or reading – you. 3rd person is used to refer to someone or somebody else – *he, she, it, they.* For example: *I* sat up. *I* was on a beach… *You* saved the budgie from the vacuum cleaner! *He* had holes in the knees of his trousers.
playscript	A playscript is the text used by actors that contains the written down version of a play. (See page 18.)
plural	(See **singular/plural** below.)
pronoun	A pronoun is a word that can replace a noun. For example: *I, me, you, he, him, she, her, we, us, it, they, them, mine, yours, his, hers, ours, theirs, its, myself, herself, himself, themselves.*
poem	A poem is a text which creates or recreates experience in a compressed and intense way, using rhythm or rhyme and language effects to create images and sound effects. (See pages 12 and 20.)
punctuation	Punctuation is the term given to those marks used to help a reader, such as full stops (.) question marks (?), commas (,), exclamation marks (!) or speech marks (' and ').
question mark	A question mark (?) is a punctuation mark that is used to end a question sentence. For example: *Did you see that, Mel?*

report	A report is a text type that provides information about a subject. (See pages 6 and 16.)
singular/ plural	Singular refers to one thing. Plural refers to more than thing. For example: *dog* (singular) sky (singular) wolf (singular) ditch (singular) *dogs* (plural) skies (plural) wolves (plural) ditches (plural)
speech marks	Speech marks (' and ') are the punctuation marks that enclose speech, including the relevant sentence punctuation. For example: *'Is that you?' she asked.* *'Dan!' cried Mrs Kane.*
speech verbs	Speech verbs are the verbs used before or after speech to show how the speech has been spoken. The most common is said. Others include – *roared, whispered, chanted, sighed.*
story	A story is a text type that recounts an invented tale. It is usually used to entertain. Stories usually have a setting, characters and are structured by a plot. (See pages 14 and 34.)
sub-heading	A sub-heading comes below a heading and indicates to the reader the content of a short section of text. For example: *Did you know…?* Before suspension systems had dampers, a car once jumped over a hedge…
tense	A tense is a verb form that shows whether events happen in the past, present or the future. Battle *is* six miles from the seaside town of Hastings. (*present tense*) The Abbey *was* built where the Battle of Hastings *took* place in 1066. (*past tense*) The firework display *will be* tremendous. (*future tense*)
title	A title is the overall heading given to a text. For example **Viking Settlers**
verb	A verb is a word that shows the action in a sentence. They are often known as 'doing' words. For example, in the following sentence the word *run* is the verb. The boys *run* down the hill.